YOUR KNOWLEDGE HAS VALUE

Patricia Alvarez Sánchez

Issues in Contemporary Literature: Black English as Identity

About Sapphari's novel "Push"

GRIN Verlag

Bibliografische Information der Deutschen Nationalbibliothek:

Die Deutsche Bibliothek verzeichnet diese Publikation in der Deutschen National-
bibliografie; detaillierte bibliografische Daten sind im Internet über http://dnb.d-
nb.de/ abrufbar.

Imprint:

Copyright © 1999 GRIN Verlag GmbH
Druck und Bindung: Books on Demand GmbH, Norderstedt Germany
ISBN: 978-3-656-48324-3

GRIN - Your knowledge has value

Der GRIN Verlag publiziert seit 1998 wissenschaftliche Arbeiten von Studenten, Hochschullehrern und anderen Akademikern als eBook und gedrucktes Buch. Die Verlagswebsite www.grin.com ist die ideale Plattform zur Veröffentlichung von Hausarbeiten, Abschlussarbeiten, wissenschaftlichen Aufsätzen, Dissertationen und Fachbüchern.

Visit us on the internet:

http://www.grin.com/

http://www.facebook.com/grincom

http://www.twitter.com/grin_com

Language as Identity

Sapphire´s Push: An example of Black English in Literature

Patricia Alvarez Sánchez
Issues in Contemporary Literature
State University of New York
March, 1999

Sapphire´s <u>Push</u>: An example of Black English in literature

Language is one very special way we have to communicate with other human beings. It unites members of similar cultures who learn to share through the same experiences and to see the world through the same vocabulary. There are at least as many cultures as languages in the world. As Wilhelm von Humboldt mentioned "The variety of languages is not merely a variety of sounds and signs, but in fact a variety of world views." Undoubtedly, languages are a unifying element that brings identity and uniqueness to every human being because they tell the rest of the world, where we come from, where we have lived and who we are.

This paper deals with Black English, also called African American English or Ebonics, as an African American linguistic variety of American English and the way it is reflected in the novel <u>Push</u> (1997) by Sapphire. It discusses Black English as a way to express and define black identity and their unique culture. There is a parallelism in the oppression of a language and the culture it represents, as we can clearly appreciate in the case of Black English. While Ebonics has been oppressed by the predominant Standard English, blacks were violently silenced by "standard" North Americans. It was not until recently that Ebonics´ uniqueness has been interpreted neither as a mispronunciation of English, nor as a series of grammatical mistakes due to ignorance or lack of education. Unfortunately, both blacks´ language and their culture have suffered from manipulation and have been bent to fit the needs of the dominant class.

Sapphari´s <u>Push</u> (1997) is a novel that combines pure poetry and brutal honesty and was also the first novel completely written in Ebonics. As such, it arose an important controversy due to its novelty and harsh themes. It tells the story of a black American adolescent who fights to survive a vicious cycle of incest and abuse. Being obese, illiterate and lacking self-esteem, her father rapes her repeatedly and she becomes pregnant for the second time, her first baby having Down´s syndrome, and is, as a result, expelled from school.

She is then sent to a special school where she meets a determined and inspiring teacher that presents himself in front of the class as being homosexual. He is proud of what he is even though he belongs to a group of people that has also been repeatedly despised and oppressed. She starts to become interested in the classes and receives the attention she really needs. He is the one that tells her she has been raped by her father, not loved, and neglected. It is through his eyes she understands it is not her own fault. She copes with her own disastrous life in terms of daydreaming, which absorbs most of her time. She dreams she is milky white, slim and desirable. With his help and encouragement, she starts reading and writing and eventually ends up writing her own poetry.

Ebonics is Precious´ first way to communicate and, in a larger sense, the way to find her unique identity throughout the novel. Ebonics is the way she has to see the world and although she is illiterate at the beginning of the novel, she is able to communicate with her most immediate world because she speaks a language she has inherited from her mother, from her ancestors and her past.

In order to understand why Precious or any other person in the United States uses a variant of English, we should consider this person´s background. Blacks speak a different variety of English because their native languages were others than English and these have deeply influenced and transformed the new language they were forced to learn. History has unfortunately shown how blacks

3

were shipped as slaves to the "New Continent", where they were treated as "merchandise". Their Black English is a response to the blending of the two languages they learned to share.

Ebonics comes from different African languages. The West African Pigdin, a Plantation Creole spoken by slaves in the United States also played a crucial role in the development of Black English. It was the language spoken on the West African coast at the time when blacks were "captured" and sold as slaves by British slave traders. This lingua franca became a creole language with the passing of time.

This language was neglected and overlooked, and still is in some areas, as a series of error productions. From a linguistic point of view, Ebonics may seem an oversimplification of English. That would happen to those unaware of its roots. It is also believed that Black English also derived from the kind of baby-talk that slave masters must have spoken to their slaves. Two instances of differences are: the loss of some suffixes, which has resulted in verbs with no tense at all; and negation, which is reduced to "ain´t" plus the meaningful verb such as in: He ain´t eat. An example of this kind of syntax is when Precious starts her story and she mentions "I ain´t eat nothing" (Sapphire, 1)

The following chart shows how West African Languages have influenced Black English in its syntax and phonology; where possible, I give examples found in <u>Push</u> (1997).

4

Syntax

Sentences do not have the verb to be	He sick today
Repetition of a noun subject with pronoun	My father, he work here
Question patterns without the auxiliary verb "do" or other auxiliaries	What it come to? Precious says: She been staring
Same form for noun in singular and plural	One boy, five boy
No tense indicated in the verb	I know it good when he ask me Precious says: Everybody call me
Same verb form for all subjects	I know, he know… Precious says: Ize gone

Phonology

General Rule in most West African Languages	Black English
No consonant pairs	Jus (for just) Mend (for mend) Precious says: Mama jus hit me wif frying pan?
Few long vowels or two part vowel (diphthongs)	Rat (for right) Tahm (for time)
No /r/ phoneme	Mow (for more)
No / ð/ phoneme	Substitution of /d/ or /f/ for /ð/ Souf (for south) Precious says: fahver

For any black children, like Precious, going to school and being taught in Standard English becomes a daily drama, especially if the teacher does not know about cultural or language differences. These children have learned Ebonics from their parents and are suddenly expected to participate in classes held in an almost foreign language to them. Moreover, they are usually thought to be "slow" students and bad learners, even though the problem lies in the fact that they are actually learning a second language. That could be one main reason why blacks tend to score poorly on IQ-Tests and especially on Verbal Tests.

The disparity comes from the fact that any black child speaking in Ebonics has to make much more effort to read and write the same a native speaker of Standard English would. Unfortunately, black children have a disadvantage that may lead them to think they have further difficulties. Such is Precious´case because she ends up feeling inferior to the rest of students. However, what may look like a disadvantage at first is actually a gift. Black children should keep their variant of English and be proud of it, because it is a proof of the richness and uniqueness of their culture.

When Precious decides to really learn Standard English, she is taking a very important step in her life. She is trying to make society accept her and she is accepting her place in a society that has kept her apart. Through her education, she is not only opening herself to the world, but also trying to "fit in with" another culture. What I personally find important is that she should not forget her first language, because it is that language the one that carries her culture and identity.

Another instance of how language shapes our mind is found in Alice in Lewis Carroll´s Through the Looking-glass (1871), where Alice is afraid to go into a wood where things lose their names and are given new ones. She says:

> This must be the wood, where things have no names. I wonder what will come of my name when I go in? I shouldn´t like to lose it all – because they´d have to give me another and it would almost certain to be an ugly one. (Carroll, 132)

Alice is a metaphor for the fear of being transformed by a second language. This is a perfect example of how language represents our identity. Her own name embeds the history of her life and background; by losing it or transforming it, she will have lost her sense of uniqueness.

We should try to fit into society to a certain point, but we should not let society completely shape us, because cultural diversity is a source of strength, creativity, and freedom. Black English is the result of two interwoven cultures that have cohabited for centuries. Therefore, it is a sign of cultural and identity enrichment that black people should be aware and proud of and preserve. When learning Standard English, Precious should preserve Ebonics as part of her black inheritance and identity.

Bibliography

- Carroll, Lewis: <u>Through the Looking-Glass</u>. New York: Dent, 1971.

- Sapphire: <u>Push</u>, New York: Vintage Contemporaries, 1997.

- Von Humboldt, Wilhelm: "On the Differentiation of the Structure of Human Language and its Effect on the Spiritual Development of the Human Race", 1830-1835 in Werke, vol. 3: <u>Schriften zur Sprachphilosophie</u>, ed. Andreas Flitner und Klaus Giel, Stuttgart: Cotta, 1963, pp 433-434.